WHO IS CUTER?

Baby Axolotl or Baby Gecko?

by Mari Schuh

BLASTOFF! READERS, AN IMPRINT OF BELLWETHER MEDIA BY FLUTTERBEE

Blastoff! Readers are carefully developed by literacy experts to build reading stamina and move students toward fluency by combining standards-based content with developmentally appropriate text.

LEVELS

Level 1 provides the most support through repetition of high-frequency words, light text, predictable sentence patterns, and strong visual support.

Level 2 offers early readers a bit more challenge through varied sentences, increased text load, and text-supportive special features.

Level 3 advances early-fluent readers toward fluency through increased text load, less reliance on photos, advancing concepts, longer sentences, and more complex special features.

★ **Blastoff! Universe**

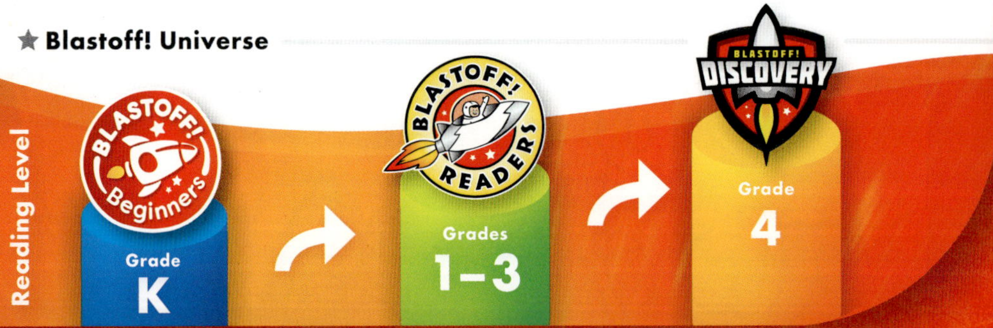

This edition first published in 2027 by Bellwether Media, Inc.

For information regarding permission, write to Bellwether Media, Inc., Attention: Permissions Department, 3500 American Blvd W, Suite 150, Bloomington, MN 55431.

Library of Congress Cataloging-in-Publication Data is available at www.loc.gov or upon request from the publisher.

ISBN: 9798898800222 (hardcover)
ISBN: 9798898801465 (ebook)

Editor: Rachael Barnes Designer: Jennifer Bowyer

Printed in the United States of America, North Mankato, MN.

Table of Contents

Babies and Eggs

Baby geckos are hatchlings. Baby axolotls are larvae.

larva
hatchling

Both babies are cute! They **hatch** from eggs. They have wide mouths.

egg

Feet and Skin

Larvae have **webbed feet**. Hatchling feet have tiny hairs. They help babies hold on.

webbed
feet

Hatchlings have soft **scales**. Larvae have wet skin.

scales

Both babies have tails. Larvae also have **fins**.

fin
tail

Water and Land

Larvae live in water.
Hatchlings live
on land.

Hatchlings use **lungs** to breathe. Larvae use lungs and **gills** to breathe.

gills

Both babies hide.
Larvae hide in mud.
Many hatchlings
hide on plants.
Who is cuter?

Who Is Cuter?

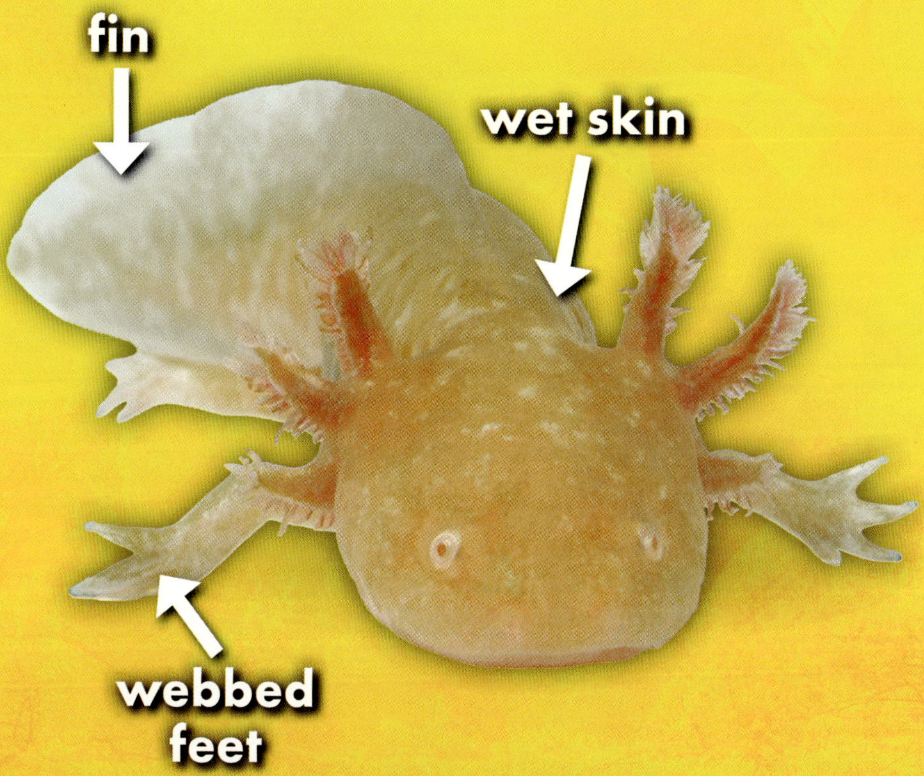

Baby Axolotl

Who is your pick?
Vote at
BellwetherMedia.com

Baby Gecko

Glossary

fins

thin body parts that help animals swim

gills

parts on axolotls that help them breathe underwater

hatch

to break out of an egg

lungs

body parts that people and animals use to breathe air

scales

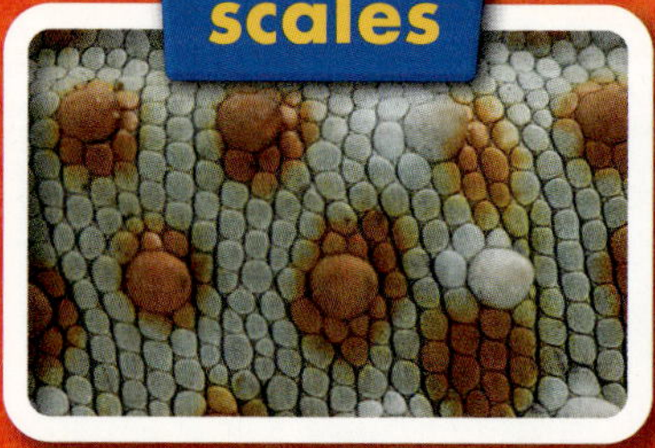

small plates that cover an animal's body

webbed feet

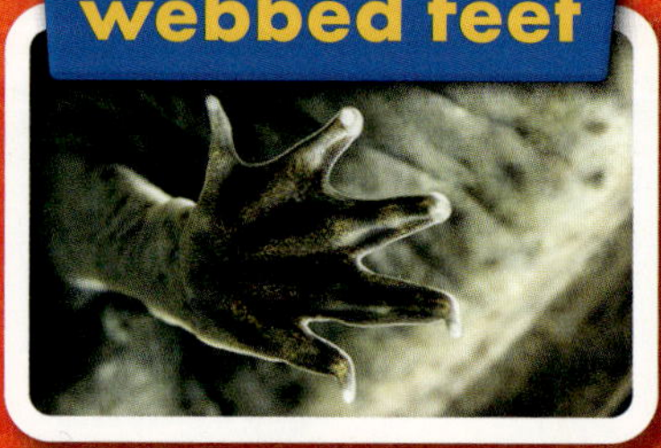

feet with thin skin between the toes

To Learn More

AT THE LIBRARY

Hansen, Grace. *Leopard Geckos in the Wild!* Minneapolis, Minn.: ABDO, 2025.

Smit, FB. *My Axolotl Life.* North Mankato, Minn.: Capstone, 2026.

Thompson, Kim. *Baby Geckos.* Mankato, Minn.: Creative Education and Creative Paperbacks, 2026.

ON THE WEB

FACTSURFER

Factsurfer.com gives you a safe, fun way to find more information.

1. Go to www.factsurfer.com.
2. Enter "baby axolotl or baby gecko" into the search box and click 🔍.
3. Select your book cover to see a list of related content.

Index

The images in this book are reproduced through the courtesy of: Raquel Pedrosa, front cover (axolotl); César Luque, front cover (gecko); Life on white/ Alamy, p. 3 (axolotl); PetlinDmitry, p. 3 (gecko); Robert Valentic/ Minden Pictures, pp. 4-5; Jan Rozehnal, pp. 5, 6-7; lessysebastian, p. 7; SylvainCDR, pp. 8-9; clicksdemexico, p. 9; Spok83, pp. 10-11; Matthijs Kuijpers/ Alamy, p. 11; Avalon.red/ Stephen Dalton/ Alamy, pp. 12-13, 22 (fins); Robert Valentic/ Minden Pictures, p. 13; Chris Mattison, pp. 14-15, 22 (hatch); N-sky, pp. 15, 20 (lives in water); rsaggin, pp. 16-17, 20 (breathes with lungs and gills), 22 (gills); Thichaa, pp. 17, 21 (breathes with lungs); Catherina Reynolds, pp. 18-19; Axolotl Photography, p. 19; Dorling Kindersley ltd/ Alamy, p. 20 (main axolotl); juanjomenta, p. 20 (hides in mud); PetlinDmitry, p. 21 (main gecko); Libin Jose, p. 21 (lives on land); Danielle Bartz/ Alamy, p. 21 (blends in); Agus_Gatam, p. 22 (lungs); dwi septiyana, p. 22 (scales); Lapis2380, p. 22 (webbed feet).